Steam Across The Northern Fells

By
Michael S. Welch

First Published 2003

ISBN 0 946184 83 6

Published By
Waterfront

A Division of Kingfisher Productions

The Dalesmade Centre, Watershed Mill, Settle,

North Yorkshire BD24 9LR

Printed by The Amadeus Press, Cleckheaton, West Yorkshire

Front cover: One wonders how many photographic masterpieces have been taken at this classic location over the years, probably thousands of pictures, but it is unlikely that many photographers were lucky enough to have the magic combination of a fairly clean locomotive and the sun shining at the same time, as seen here. What a pity the leading engine is not emitting a little bit more smoke, to really enhance the picture, but the locomotive's fireman was clearly doing his job correctly, note the safety valves lifting slightly, so one should not complain, well, not much! The location is, of course, Shap Wells, and the train is a northbound freight hauled by Class 7P 'Patriot' No. 45527 *Southport* and banked by Fairburn 2-6-4T No. 42110. This picture was taken on 1st September 1964. Today, the well-known Shap Wells mound, where generations of photographers stood to record the scene, has been covered by conifer trees, so it is no longer possible to take a shot at this location. *Alan Robey*

Back cover: The increasing dieselisation of BR in the 1960s frequently resulted in the relegation of steam locomotives to secondary duties and the maintenance of the fleet was hardly the motive power department's top priority. Needless to say, the external cleanliness of many locomotives left much to be desired, as many of the pictures in this album bear ample testament, and even once-proud express passenger engines were often seen in grimy condition. Of course, there were exceptions to this rule and in this illustration a respectably clean Stanier Class 6P5F 'Jubilee' 4-6-0, No. 45584 *North West Frontier*, has steam to spare as it rounds the curve at Grayrigg with a northbound parcels train on 1st September 1964. The photographer probably could not believe his good fortune! At the time of this picture No. 45584 was one of a handful of these locomotives based at Blackpool shed and was presumably the pride of the depot. *Alan Robey*

Title page: This picture of Stanier Class 5MT No. 45231 heading a local ballast train near Grange-over-Sands on 1st August 1968 contains nothing to suggest that the end was nigh. It was probably nothing more than a routine job for the crew. Despite the inescapable fact that the end of steam traction was a few days away when this scene was recorded, it was almost 'business' as usual at the remaining steam depots right up to the last day, almost as if they were unaware that steam was doomed. Only the ever-lengthening lines of withdrawn engines suggested that the end of an era was approaching. At Carnforth shed, steam locomotives were booked on their usual local freight and ballast duties during the last week, and it is recorded that these included turns to Preston, Barrow-in-Furness, Windermere and Heysham, in addition to the more local work seen here. But if an observer had returned a week later he would have had a nasty shock; No. 45231 would have been cold on Carnforth shed while the ballast train would have produced an unappealing diesel. *David Clark*

This page: An evening freight from Carlisle to West Cumberland, powered by Fowler Class 4F 0-6-0 No. 44399, crosses the River Caldew at Cummersdale on 13th August 1962. The train includes a couple of milk tankers to be returned to Aspatria creamery. It is hard to believe that this most delightful rural location is only a couple of miles from the centre of Carlisle. There used to be a station at Cummersdale, which is probably best described as a Carlisle 'suburban' station, but it closed on 18th June 1951. No. 44399 was one of a batch of these engines built by the North British Locomotive Company, being outshopped in December 1926. It remained in service until withdrawal occurred in February 1964. *Robert Leslie*

Introduction

The railways across the northern fells have always had a special appeal and fascination, largely due to the fact that they traverse inhospitable mountainous terrain and encountered daunting natural obstacles during construction. The result was a series of outstanding, incomparable routes passing through some of the most magnificent landscapes in Great Britain. In addition, they have had a high profile because of the popularity of the Shap route, and to a lesser extent the Settle & Carlisle line, with railway photographers. In the 1950s/60s railway periodicals were liberally sprinkled with photographic masterpieces taken by the late Eric Treacy and the late Derek Cross. The superb landscape and memorable sight of steam engines working hard were, after all, the perfect combination for a stunning picture, especially if the sun deigned to appear at the critical moment!

Stanier Class 4MT 2-6-4T No. 42449 stands in Platform Two at Windermere station with an unidentified train on 3rd August 1964. Those coaches in the train that can be seen are of LMSR origin. The station's decorative, and very distinctive, overall roof is visible on the extreme left while the substantial stone-built goods shed stands out above the first coach of the train. The picture is completed by an attractive terrace of houses, and a pleasant backdrop of trees.

Chris Gammell

Undoubtedly, the best-known route through the fells is the West Coast Main Line (WCML), a very busy main traffic artery. In steam days the heavier trains required banking assistance from Oxenholme to Grayrigg and also from Tebay to Shap summit. The sight and sound of a heavy northbound train, with locomotives on the front and at the rear, toiling up Shap incline was one of the finest displays of raw steam power in Great Britain and an absolutely unforgettable experience. Until the coming of the diesels, fast expresses on this route were often powered by 'Princess Coronation' Class Pacifics, which were arguably the finest express passenger steam locomotives ever to run in Great Britain.

The premature withdrawal of the remaining members of the class in September 1964, when many engines were still in quite reasonable mechanical condition, was a sad event. Despite the demise of those impressive machines, steam traction continued to work over Shap until the end of 1967, the final BR passenger working apparently being a return Carlisle to Blackpool football special on Boxing Day hauled by 'Britannia' Class 7P6F Pacific No. 70013 *Oliver Cromwell*. A great deal has been written over the years about the splendours of the Settle & Carlisle line, an epic, legendary route which has caught the imagination of generations of railway aficionados. Despite its fantastic scenery, the S&C never seemed to attract photographers in the same numbers as the Shap route, perhaps due to its lighter traffic density and the lure of the 'Princess Coronation' Pacifics on the latter line. Understandably, perhaps, enthusiasts preferred a sparkling Stanier Pacific at the head of a heavy train over Shap to a dirty 'Black Five' on an occasional S&C line freight. During the summer of 1967, however, the last 'Jubilee' Class locomotives were regularly rostered to work over the S&C route on summer Saturday extra trains and attracted many observers.

In many respects the most remarkable line covered by this album is the lengthy Carnforth-Barrow-Carlisle route. This route is something of a backwater, but offers much of interest, including long viaducts across wide estuaries, superb views where is skirts the Lake District and a number of separate single line sections on this otherwise double track line. North of Whitehaven, the route twists and turns as it follows the coastline, before reaching Workington, which was best known for its traditional coal and steel industries.

The Stainmore line, which reaches a height of 1,370 feet above sea level, is another intriguing route covered by this album. This was a line of fearsome gradients and some remarkable engineering works, such as Belah viaduct. Interestingly, following the closure of the Kirkby Stephen to Tebay line to advertised passenger trains in the early 1950s, this route continued to be used by summer Saturday workings from the North East to Blackpool for a further ten years. How infinitely more interesting the railway system was in those days compared to today! Other routes featured in this book include the C.K. & P.R., which boasted some breathtaking Lake District scenery, and the often neglected Windermere branch.

It has been a great pleasure compiling this album and I hope that readers will derive some enjoyment from the pages that follow, if so it has been a thoroughly worthwhile exercise. Grateful thanks are due to the many photographers who have so kindly trusted me with their slides, to Chris Evans and David J. Fakes who kindly read the manuscript and, of course, to my publisher, Roger Hardingham.

M.S.Welch, Burgess Hill, West Sussex January 2003

Stanier Class 5MT No. 44763 emits a volcanic smoke effect, and disturbs the peace of Oxenholme station, as it blasts through with a down freight on the morning of 1st September 1964. The tracks of the Windermere branch can just be discerned in the shadows behind the locomotive. Like many of its sister engines, No. 44763 was a product of Crewe Works, from where it emerged in October 1947. It lasted in traffic for exactly one year after this shot was taken.

Alan Robey

One can only imagine the deafening noise being produced by BR Standard Class 9F No. 92017 as it heaves a long northbound freight up Grayrigg bank on a sunny 1st September 1964. In the early 1960s many Class 9Fs could be found on heavy freight haulage in the Midlands, both Annesley and Wellingborough sheds having a substantial allocation. In addition, Doncaster shed had a sizeable number while they were also common in South Wales. When they became surplus to requirements in these areas they were frequently transferred to the LMR for duty on the West Coast Main Line, where they became a regular sight during the last years of steam. No. 92017, however, spent much of its career at Newton Heath shed, Manchester, and was withdrawn in December 1967 from Carlisle Kingmoor shed when steam traction finished in that city.

Alan Robey

Fortunately for the enginemen, No. 92017 was not expected to tackle the climb unassisted, Oxenholme providing Fowler 2-6-4T No. 42414 as a banker which is seen in this shot pushing mightily at the rear. The 2-6-4T was not destined to last much longer on these duties after this photograph was taken, being withdrawn during October 1964 after almost 31 years' service.

Alan Robey

A stranger in the fells! It may seem almost unbelievable, but the location of this photograph is Grayrigg bank, and the date is 13th June 1964 when the Railway Correspondence & Travel Society ran their 'Solway Ranger' railtour. The star attraction was Bulleid 'Merchant Navy' Class Pacific No. 35012 *United States Lines*, which was booked to haul the train from Leeds (City) to Penrith via Carnforth (reverse) on the outward leg, and all of the way back from Carlisle to Leeds via the S&C line. The locomotive was driven by the late Bert Hooker, a renowned 'Southern' engineman. No. 35012 is seen here making light work of Grayrigg bank, where the summit was reportedly passed at 60mph! After arrival at Penrith the participants journeyed along the exceptionally scenic route through the heart of the Lake District to Workington. Most of the passengers left the main train at Workington and boarded a d.m.u. for (what must have been) a fascinating exploration of various obscure goods-only lines in the area. These included visits to Rowrah and a trip over the Moor Row to Sellafield line. Later in the day, participants were hauled over the Silloth branch by a couple of the Scottish Region's preserved locomotives. One would have thought that this would have been enough excitement for one day, but the best was yet to come. *United States Lines* was booked to take the train back to Leeds via Settle, and gave a memorable performance. Armathwaite was passed at 70mph and from thereon No. 35012 ran like an engine possessed. Appleby was reached in 42.02 minutes and the ensuing 17.45 miles-long climb to Ais Gill was completed in 17.41 minutes, the summit being breasted at more than 60mph, a truly magnificent performance, to conclude a splendid day out.

Alan Robey

A sad moment in history as Stanier 'Princess Coronation' Class 8P Pacific No. 46237 *City of Bristol* approaches Lambrigg crossing, on the climb towards Grayrigg summit, with a down parcels train on 13th September 1964. Note the plume of white steam at the rear of the tender, indicating that the coal pusher was in use. Apart from No. 46256 *Sir William A. Stanier, F.R.S.*, which was retained for a few extra weeks for railtour duties, all surviving members of this celebrated class were officially withdrawn from 12th September, though at the time it was reported that one or two locomotives remained in service for a few days after that date. Presumably No. 46237 was one of those engines that evaded the official withdrawal deadline, so it is likely that this was *City of Bristol*'s last ever revenue-earning duty and it was immediately taken out of service on arrival at Carlisle Upperby shed. Like its sister engines which ended their working careers at Carlisle, No. 46237 was sold for scrap to the West of Scotland Shipbreaking Company of Troon, Ayrshire, where it was laid to rest in December 1964.

Alan Robey

In this stirring action shot, taken at Mosedale Hall crossing just south of Grayrigg summit, the 9.30am Manchester Victoria to Glasgow Central train is seen ascending the bank behind Class 7P 'Patriot' No. 45531 *Sir Frederick Harrison* piloted by Class 4P 2-6-4T No. 42449. If a pilot locomotive was taken at Oxenholme it normally worked through to Shap summit, whereas a banking engine would travel only as far as Grayrigg summit and then return to Oxenholme. The gradient at this point is 1 in 106, this being the steepest section of the bank, apart from a very brief stretch of 1 in 104. This shot was taken on 13th September 1964.

Alan Robey

Breasting the summit at Grayrigg! The enginemen on the footplate of Stanier Class 5MT No. 44899 pose for the photographer as they pass the site of Grayrigg station with a Morecambe to Glasgow relief on 1st August 1964. They had every reason to relax for a short time, because the train had just surmounted the summit after nearly twenty miles of almost continuous climbing from Carnforth, and their locomotive appears to be going extremely well, with hardly a trace of leaking steam at the front end, and a splendid smokescreen. The fireman would soon have been busy again, however, building up boiler pressure for the gruelling climb up to Shap summit. Some of the remains of Grayrigg station, which was closed in February 1954, are visible.

Alan Chandler

Photographed on a bright and sunny 1st September 1964, Stanier Class 6P5F 'Jubilee' 4-6-0 No. 45567 *South Australia* eases a down freight out of the loop at Grayrigg. There are loops on both the up and down lines at Grayrigg, the up loop being located near the signal box which is just visible in the distance. No. 45567 was constructed by the North British Locomotive Co. of Glasgow in August 1934 and had only five months of life remaining when this scene was recorded.

Alan Robey

Right top: A southbound freight headed by 'Black Five' No. 45317, rounds the sharp curve at the former Low Gill station on 14th April 1962. The line visible on the right was the branch to Ingleton and Clapham Junction, which provided a direct connection to Skipton and the West Riding. In times gone by Midland Railway (MR) passengers travelling to Scotland were obliged to change trains here, and were hardly made welcome by the rival London & North Western Railway, sometimes being conveyed between Low Gill and Carlisle in carriages attached to the rear of slow moving goods trains. The proud MR was outraged that its passengers were being treated in such a manner and vowed to build its own, independent route to Scotland. This resulted in the construction of the magnificent Settle & Carlisle line (S&C line), which was opened in 1876. Following the opening of the S&C line, the Low Gill to Clapham section, which served a thinly populated area of scattered rural communities, declined in status. A through Leeds to Keswick service operated for a short time, but a paltry service of four local trains a day was usually sufficient to cater for the few passengers who remained. The line's regular passenger trains were withdrawn from 1st February 1954, but occasional schools trains and freight workings continued to operate after that date. Despite the line's undoubted usefulness as a diversionary route, the harsh economic realities of the 1960s precluded its retention for such purposes, and it was shut completely in July 1966. Despite its isolated position, miles from a settlement of any importance, Low Gill station survived long after the closure of the Ingleton branch, not closing until 7th March 1960. *Alan Robey*

Right bottom: BR Standard 'Britannia' Pacific No. 70051 *Firth of Forth* races through the Lune Gorge with an unidentified southbound passenger working in July 1967. This is almost certainly a summer Saturday extra from Glasgow to Morecambe or Blackpool. In 1970 this magnificent stretch of countryside was ruined by the construction of the M6 motorway which has had a much more intrusive effect on the landscape than the railway. *Derek Huntriss*

The fireman of Class 9F 2-10-0 No. 92017 seems to very hard at work, building up the fire for the ascent of Shap, as it passes through the Lune Gorge and approaches Tebay with a heavy northbound freight in the mid-1960s. Surprisingly, very few pictures of trains threading the Lune Gorge were submitted for inclusion in this album, presumably because most photographers visiting the area preferred the drama and excitement of observing trains blasting up the 1 in 75 towards Shap summit.

Maurice Burns

In this wonderfully evocative picture, the driver of 'Princess Coronation' Pacific No. 46225 *Duchess of Gloucester* is seen in classic pose, waiting for the guard to give him the 'right away' at Tebay on 31st May 1963. The identity of the train is unknown, but it is almost certainly an early morning stopping train which left Carlisle at about 6.15am. In the winter 1964 timetable it was advertised to leave Carlisle at 6.20am and call at all stations to Crewe, except Garstang & Catterall, where it was booked to arrive at 11.24am. The incredibly long journey time is partially explained by the fact that the train usually waited for at least ten minutes at each principal station. The locomotive's unkempt condition will be noted. By this time the remaining 'Duchesses', as they were commonly known, could often be found on seasonal passenger workings and various menial tasks, as seen here.
Chris Gammell

The sombre black clouds, distant fells dappled by sunshine, cows and sheep grazing contentedly and the superb spectacle of a northbound freight train doing battle with the 1 in 75 gradient past Greenholme. There were few locations on the BR network where the raw power of steam traction could be experienced in such a magnificent, breathtaking setting as the northern fells between Oxenholme and Shap summit. The surrounding fields north of Tebay, for example, provided an ideal grandstand from where to observe and photograph trains as they blasted upgrade, frequently assisted in the rear, as seen here in this portrait taken on 31st July 1965.

Alan Robey

On the evening of 1st September 1964 the fells around Tebay - were bathed in superb golden sunshine, so imagine the photographer's huge joy when he heard the sound of two locomotives exchanging whistles down at Tebay - a steam train was on its way! His joy probably turned to considerable disappointment as the train engine, Stanier 'Jubilee' 4-6-0 No. 45617 *Mauritius*, in indescribably filthy condition, passed his vantage point at Greenholme without emitting even a trace of exhaust, thus ruining a potentially stunning masterpiece. But the banking engine, Fairburn 2-6-4T No. 42110, which is seen here, duly obliged with a reasonable smoke effect. Usually the engine at the front of the train is in the starring role, while the banker occupies only a supporting part. For once the positions are reversed!

Alan Robey

Above: The sight and sound of a 'Royal Scot' locomotive climbing Shap at the head of an Anglo-Scottish express had been an everyday event for many years, but by the time this picture was taken, on 31st July 1965, it had become exceedingly rare. Only five 'Royal Scots' lasted into 1965, and by the time of this picture just two engines, Nos. 46115 and 46140, remained active. In this shot No. 46115 *Scots Guardsman* is seen at Shap Wells with the 1.12pm Liverpool to Glasgow train. The enginemen presumably had considerable confidence in their locomotive's capabilities because they opted to tackle the incline unaided, or maybe there wasn't a banker available at Tebay! During the ensuing three months No. 46115 was active on a wide range of duties, but by 5th November it was out of use, apparently 'stopped' for repair at Carlisle Kingmoor shed, and was withdrawn a few weeks later. Its last reported duty was the 4.45pm Glasgow St. Enoch to Carlisle parcels train on 20th October. *Scots Guardsman* was subsequently preserved, but has rarely been in operational condition.

Alan Chandler

Left: The magnificent, unforgettable spectacle of steam locomotives climbing towards Shap summit. In this view, taken from the eastern side of the line, an unidentified Stanier Class 5MT 4-6-0, assisted at the rear by a BR Standard Class 4MT 4-6-0, plods up the 1 in 75 past Scout Green some time in 1967. The cleft in the hills in the far distance indicates the course taken by the railway through the Lune Gorge. In the late 1830s a government commission suggested that a line skirting the eastern fringe of the Lake District would be the best route for a railway between Oxenholme and Carlisle, and proposed a tunnel under Orton Scar. In the event the promoters decided to save time and money by taking the line straight over Shap without a tunnel, a rash decision creating the Shap incline which has handicapped operations over the line ever since.

Maurice Burns

A light dusting of snow, a brilliant clear, blue sky and a heavy freight train blasting up to Shap summit behind a 'Black Five', with a 2-6-4T assisting at the rear. Sometimes railway photographers are fortunate enough to obtain just the right conditions and a masterpiece results, as seen here. The location is, of course, Shap Wells and this picture was taken on 28th November 1964. Need any more be said?

Maurice Burns

Stanier 'Princess Coronation' Pacific No. 46254 *City of Stoke-on-Trent* powers the 12.52pm Euston to Glasgow St. Enoch at Shap Wells on 1st August 1964. The photographer comments that the driver of No. 46254 had just shut off steam, apparently because it had just caught up a preceding diesel! This train was a summer Saturday relief working, presumably to the 'Mid-Day Scot', which only ran on peak Saturdays as required. In the days prior to the implementation of the Beeching Plan, BR still maintained a substantial pool of coaches in order to cater for surges of traffic at peak periods and all of the vehicles formed in this train, like the engine hauling them, appear to be of LMSR design. Sadly, *City of Stoke-on-Trent* was laid aside on 12th September 1964, but not before it had a final fling working the down 'Mid-Day Scot' on 29th August.

Alan Chandler

After almost four miles of continuous climbing, the top of the bank is almost in sight for the crew of Stanier 'Black Five' No. 45253, powering a freight working, as it passes through the deep cutting just before Shap summit is reached. This picture was taken on 10th June 1967. No. 45253 was among the total of 327 of these machines built by Armstrong Whitworth & Co., this particular example being constructed in September 1936. It survived in traffic until the last year of BR standard gauge steam, being taken out of service in March 1968.   *Alan Robey*

During the final months of steam traction at Carlisle, the vast majority of Kingmoor shed's locomotives were in absolutely deplorable external condition, but there is always an exception, and here it is! A smartly turned-out BR Standard Class 7P6F 'Britannia' Pacific, No. 70038 *Robin Hood*, is seen starting the descent from Shap summit, which is hidden by the smoke towards the rear of the train. The 'Britannia' was working the 2.00pm Glasgow to Liverpool train on 22nd July 1967. Note the enthusiasts travelling in the front coach: let us hope that No. 70038 gave them a good run!

Peter Fitton

The 2.00pm Glasgow Central to Liverpool Exchange express arrives at Penrith on 1st August 1964 behind a pair of Stanier-designed 4-6-0s, 'Jubilee' No. 45742 *Connaught* piloted by 'Black Five' No. 45055. Both locomotives are 'blowing off' in preparation for the climb to Shap summit which lies ahead. Penrith first appeared on the railway map in December 1846 when trains started running from Lancaster to Carlisle. Note the bay platform on the left, which was used by trains to Keswick and Workington.

Chris Gammell

Right: The setting sun beautifully illuminates a southbound freight, hauled by an unidentified Stanier Class 5MT 4-6-0, as it heads past Southwaite on the evening of 25th May 1963. What better lighting conditions could a railway photographer wish for? There used to be a station at Southwaite, but is was closed as long ago as 7th April 1952.   *Robert Leslie*

Left: Hughes/Fowler Class 5MT 2-6-0 No. 42777 takes a southbound freight from Kingmoor yard up the 1 in 131 climb from Carlisle to Wreay on the evening of 22nd May 1963. Note that the train includes a number of cattle wagons. These locomotives had a particularly high running plate which gave them a rather ungainly appearance and consequently they were nicknamed 'Crabs'. A total of 245 of these 2-6-0s was built between 1926 and 1932 and the last of these robust and workmanlike machines was not withdrawn until early 1967. They were generally extremely popular with enginemen due to them being sure-footed while working uphill. No. 42777 was a product of Crewe Works, from where it emerged in August 1927, and it remained in traffic until August 1965.   *Robert Leslie*

Left: The shadows are lengthening on the glorious evening of 19th April 1963, as Stanier Class 8F 2-8-0 No. 48108 plods southwards past the former Brisco station with a freight from Kingmoor yard. The station building was one of many on the northern section of the West Coast Main Line designed by the noted Victorian architect William Tite. Unfortunately, the station must have been one of the shortest lived anywhere. It was closed in 1852, six years after the line opened, a replacement station at nearby Wreay being brought into use during the following year. *Robert Leslie*

Right: The light covering of snow on the ground makes a perfect Christmas card scene at Brisco on 29th December 1962, as BR Standard Class 7P6F 'Britannia' Pacific No. 70028 *Royal Star* passes the old station with an Edinburgh to Birmingham express. No. 70028 began life at Cardiff Canton shed, on the Western Region, in December 1952 and remained there until it was ousted by diesels. It moved to Aston shed, Birmingham, in October 1961 and then spent the remainder of its career on the LMR at a variety of depots including both Crewe sheds, Longsight (Manchester), Llandudno Junction and Willesden. Its final transfer took place in October 1966 from which time it was based at Carlisle Kingmoor shed until withdrawal occurred in September 1967. *Robert Leslie*

Stanier Class 8P 'Princess Coronation' Pacific No. 46225 *Duchess of Gloucester* makes a fine sight as it gets into its stride with a Glasgow to Birmingham express. It was photographed passing Carlisle No. 13 signalbox at Upperby on Easter Monday, 15th April 1963. Apart from two brief respites, the line southwards from Carlisle climbs for 31 miles until Shap summit is reached, so the fireman would have had some hard work to do! Note that this stretch of line was still mechanically signalled at this time. A new signalbox was constructed at the south end of Carlisle station in 1951, but this only controlled part of the station area and the signal box seen here presumably survived until a new power signalbox was commissioned at Carlisle in 1973 prior to electrification. It is, perhaps, surprising that mechanical signalling lasted for so long on this section of the important West Coast Main Line.

Robert Leslie

Railway working in the Carlisle area was, of course, dominated by LMSR types, but there was a small enclave of LNER-designed locomotives at the former North British Railway's Canal shed. This was located in the 'vee' formed by the junction of the Edinburgh and Silloth lines, north of the city. It was the smallest of the Carlisle sheds, but in many ways was the most interesting, its allocation in the early 1960s consisting mainly of B1 Class 4-6-0s, K3 Class 2-6-0s, J39 0-6-0s and even one or two ancient NBR J36 Class 0-6-0s. The pride of the shed, though, was probably its quartet of A3 Pacifics used on Waverley route passenger turns. In this picture J39 Class 0-6-0 No. 64877 is depicted in May 1961 at Upperby, somewhat removed from its usual haunts on the north side of the city, hauling (what appears to be) a train of empty coaches from a Silloth service.

George M. Staddon/Colour-Rail

Memories of the glorious days of steam are superbly recaptured in this glimpse of the up 'Caledonian' pausing at Carlisle station on 15th June 1958. Motive power is provided by Stanier 'Princess Coronation' Pacific No. 46239 *City of Chester* which is in exemplary external condition. This train was introduced between London and Glasgow by the LMR and ScR in 1957, following the success of the 'Talisman' on the East Coast Route. It offered a very fast service between the two cities, stopping only at Carlisle in each direction, and was limited to only eight coaches. In the early 1960s further stops were introduced and as a result of electrification work the train was withdrawn altogether in the autumn of 1964, after a relatively short career.

Neil Thexton

In this portrait taken at Carlisle station on 23rd February 1963, Ivatt-designed Class 2MT No. 46491 undertakes some shunting of empty coaching stock whilst on station pilot duty, a task that is unlikely to have over-exerted the 'Mogul'. In times gone by, owing to the large number of pre-grouping companies working into Carlisle, there was a station committee which co-ordinated the management of the station. Even into the 1950s Carlisle station, which was previously known as 'Carlisle Citadel', retained the atmosphere of a frontier station, where Anglo-Scottish expresses usually changed engines, those of the LMR giving way to ScR locomotives. In 1957/58 the huge overall roof was reduced in size, the distinctive Gothic end screens being removed at the same time. During the 1950s and early 1960s three engine sheds were still operational, and it is estimated that 4,000 people in Carlisle worked on the railway, underlining the city's status as a major traffic centre. *Robert Leslie*

A scene at the north end of Carlisle station on 15th May 1960 showing Gresley Class A3 Pacific No. 60093 *Coronach* apparently awaiting departure with a train to Edinburgh via the Waverley route. The driver is sitting on the running plate topping up the mechanical lubricator. Considerable efforts had obviously been made by the cleaners at Carlisle Canal shed to spruce up the locomotive, but clearly, judging by the large areas of the engine still coated with a liberal covering of grime, they ran out of time! *Coronach* was built in December 1928 as LNER No. 2747 and was withdrawn from traffic in April 1962. It was one of a small number of this class that spent a long period allocated to Carlisle Canal shed for use on the Waverley route and hardly ever appeared in London, much to the frustration of train spotters in the Capital. Its low profile doubtless ensured that is was one of the least photographed members of the class, so this colour portrait may be quite a rarity.

Chris Gammell

Stanier Class 8P 'Princess Royal' Pacific No. 46203 *Princess Margaret Rose* makes an evocative and stirring sight as it approaches Etterby Junction, north of Carlisle, on 8th September 1962. The train is unidentified, but it is almost certainly the 10.00am Euston to Perth which was regularly rostered for a Carlisle Pacific at this time. Sadly, this is likely to have been No. 46203's final appearance in revenue-earning service. In early 1961 the entire class had been placed in store, but many reappeared in service during the summer of that year. This reprieve was only temporary for some members of the class, however, as six examples were condemned in the autumn. The survivors returned to store, but were surprisingly re-instated to traffic in January 1962 as a result of a motive power shortage. On 10th September 1962 five 'Princess Royals', including No. 46203, were put back into store, the only exception being No. 46200 *The Princess Royal* which remained active. The five stored engines were condemned during the following month, while No. 46200 followed shortly afterwards. So the careers of these impressive machines came to an end, almost thirty years after their introduction.

Geoff Rixon

Judging by the clouds of black smoke being emitted, the fireman of Class 7P 'Patriot' No. 45527 *Southport* is already hard at work for the climb ahead as it passes Etterby Junction with a Manchester to Glasgow express on 28th June 1964. Note the first three coaches formed immediately behind the engine are all of LNER origin, the first being a Gresley-designed brake vehicle, while the next two vehicles are later Thompson coaches. *Robert Leslie*

Stanier Class 5MT 4-6-0 No. 45122 rattles over the crossovers at Etterby Junction with an unidentified southbound passenger working on 1st June 1957. Note that the short train includes a LMSR twelve-wheeled restaurant car in its formation. In the background the massive Kingmoor engine shed, or motive power depot to give it its official title, can be seen, beneath the continuous pall of smoke which always seemed to hang over the premises. The huge concrete structure on the right is the shed's mechanical coaling plant. In early 1967 a total of 129 steam locomotives was allocated to Kingmoor shed, including 30 'Britannia' Pacifics and two dozen Class 9Fs, but by the end of that year rapid dieselisation had rendered steam traction redundant and the depot closed on 31st December. This brought to an end steam working over the Shap and Settle & Carlisle routes.

Trevor Owen

BR Standard Class 7P6F 'Britannia' Pacific No. 70010 *Owen Glendower*, in extremely neglected external condition, eases a southbound freight out of Kingmoor marshalling yard, north of Carlisle, in October 1966. Construction of the yard received high priority in the BR modernisation plan, parliamentary authority to purchase the land being given in 1956, and preparatory work commenced in 1959. Unfortunately, over 400 acres of mainly arable land were lost to agriculture. This colossal £4½ million project, which occupied a site on the western side of the main line to Scotland, involved an area 2½ miles-long by ¼ mile wide. The yard was designed to handle 5,600 wagons a day and boasted 123 roads covering 56 track miles. The whole area was floodlit at night by fifteen 150ft high towers. Special connections had to be laid to enable trains to reach the Waverley route to Edinburgh. The yard was completed in 1963, this also being the year, by a most unfortunate coincidence, that the Beeching Report was published. The report foreshadowed a change of policy from wagonload traffic to block trains and also recommended closure of the Waverley route. The yard proved to be a total white elephant which never reached its potential and parts of the complex were closed as early as 1972. *Derek Huntriss*

Right: Photographed on a sunny August afternoon in 1962, Stanier 'Royal Scot' 4-6-0 No. 46127 *Old Contemptibles* pauses at Hellifield with the afternoon Bradford Forster Square to Carlisle train, which stopped at all stations north of Hellifield. In the summer 1959 timetable this working left Bradford at 3.40pm and reached Hellifield at 4.43pm, where it presumably stopped for water. It was booked to leave there at 5.05pm and its advertised arrival time at Carlisle was 7.29pm. Even by the standards of the time the train had an extremely leisurely schedule: 76 miles in just under 2½ hours was hardly demanding, but on a beautiful summer's evening with the S&C line's magnificent scenery at its best, would any passenger complain? No. 46127 was built in 1927 and rebuilt with a 2A type taper boiler in 1944. By the time of this picture it had been relegated to less exacting duties and lasted only a further six months in service after this shot was taken. *K.J. MacDonald/Colour-Rail*

Left: The 8.05am Carlisle to Hellifield train, hauled by BR Standard Class 6P5F Pacific No. 72006, is seen leaving Horton-in-Ribblesdale on a sunny 15th May 1965. This machine was formerly named *Clan Mackenzie*, but by the time of this photograph its nameplates had been removed. These engines, which were commonly known as 'Clans', were nicely proportioned, but were not particularly powerful for their size and were frequently criticised for their indifferent steaming characteristics. There had been plans to build around 25 'Clans', but in the event only ten locomotives were constructed, these being shared between Kingmoor (Carlisle) and Polmadie (Glasgow) sheds. Before their principal duties were taken over by diesels in the early 1960s, the Polmadie-based 'Clans' could often be found on the Glasgow to Liverpool/Manchester expresses, while the Carlisle locomotives regularly powered services to Glasgow, Aberdeen and Stranraer. The engines allocated to Polmadie were condemned *en masse* in December 1962, but the Kingmoor engines remained in service much longer, not being withdrawn until heavy repairs became due. *Alan Chandler*

A classic S&C line photograph! In this memorable scene Stanier Class 6P5F 'Jubilee' 4-6-0 No. 45697 *Achilles* pulls a northbound freight across Ribblehead viaduct in superb early morning light on 26th August 1966. Construction of this twenty-four arch, 440 yards-long viaduct began in October 1870 and was finished in 1875. It was an achievement of Victorian engineering and has stood firm against the very severe weather which prevails in these parts. At one time more than two thousand navvies were employed on the construction work, being housed in hutted camps adjacent to the line. They often laboured in appalling conditions, the incessant rain and fierce winds sometimes forcing work to be halted until the weather improved. Sadly, many men perished during the work and were laid to rest in the churchyard at nearby Chapel-le-Dale, where a plaque was erected to commemorate those who died. The mountain in the background is Ingleborough, one of the three peaks for which this area is famous. Roy *Hobbs*

Stanier Class 5MT 4-6-0 No. 44667 climbs towards Blea Moor with the afternoon Bradford Forster Square to Carlisle stopping train in July 1965. This train was usually formed of three coaches plus a few miscellaneous vans, so it was probably one of the easiest turns over the S&C line and is certainly unlikely to have taxed No. 44667 unduly. This machine was amongst the last members of this very large class, which totalled 842 locomotives, to be constructed. It was released from Crewe Works in July 1949 and lasted until September 1967.

Maurice Burns

In the author's view the stretch of line through Dentdale is the prettiest on the entire S&C line, and here a southbound freight headed by 'Black Five' No. 44727 is seen crossing Dent Head viaduct on a sunny 22nd July 1967. The course of the railway through Dentdale can be clearly seen as it runs along the lower slopes of Widdale Fell. Note Dent Head signal box, which was still *in situ* despite being out of use by the date of this picture. The remains of a row of snow fences, which were installed to protect the tracks from the worst Pennine blizzards, can also be picked out together with the position of Dent station, on the extreme left, indicated by a light-coloured building.

Peter Fitton

Left: When a batch of Gresley Class A3 Pacifics was allocated to Leeds Holbeck shed in early 1960, for use on Anglo-Scottish trains via the S&C line, the reaction of the shed staff and enginemen was probably one of total incredulity. After all, Holbeck shed had a long LMSR tradition and the A3s must have seemed almost completely alien. Despite their somewhat neglected mechanical condition, the newcomers soon found favour amongst the men due to their free-steaming characteristics and extremely comfortable cabs. By November 1960 a total of nine locomotives was based at Holbeck and it is doubtful whether the shed had previously boasted such a sizeable allocation of large express passenger engines. The A3s probably found the demanding S&C line a much sterner test than the racing ground of the East Coast Main Line! Unfortunately, the class's domination of the S&C line's expresses was destined to be short-lived, because BR/Sulzer diesels were drafted in during June 1961, but A3s continued to make fitful appearances for a couple of years afterwards. In this illustration No. 60080 *Dick Turpin*, in dreadful external condition, is seen picking up water as it heads the down 'Waverley' over Garsdale troughs on 5th September 1960, a typically dull and murky Pennine day.   *Trevor Owen*

Right: A southbound freight, powered by Stanier Class 5MT 4-6-0 No. 45186, approaches Garsdale on 22nd August 1967. The locomotive is in extremely unkempt condition, particularly the smokebox which is disfigured by spots of what appears to be white paint, but is more likely a deposit caused by severe priming. Note the unusual vehicle marshalled immediately behind the locomotive which is similar to a nuclear flask wagon. The trackbed of the branch line to Hawes and Northallerton is prominent in the foreground. The Garsdale to Hawes line was opened by the MR in 1878 following the arrival at Hawes of the North Eastern Railway's branch from Northallerton. This line served a very thinly populated area and the last train ran from Garsdale to Northallerton on 24th April 1954. The short link from Garsdale to Hawes survived until March 1959.
Alan Chandler

A panoramic view, taken near Garsdale station on 5th September 1960, of Dandry Mire viaduct looking towards Moorcock tunnel, with Class 4F 0-6-0 No. 43908 pottering across the viaduct with a short pick-up goods train. Perhaps Garsdale's famous stockaded turntable, in the foreground, will be of greater interest. At one time Garsdale was the point at which pilot locomotives were detached from both northbound and southbound trains, and the turntable was installed by the MR in order to turn engines waiting to return to their home shed. Not even the hardiest locomotive crew would have wanted to travel back home tender-first on a stormy Pennine night! There is an old tale of a locomotive being caught by the wind as it was being turned and it apparently spun out of control for several hours afterwards. In order to stop a repeat of this remarkable event a stockade, formed of old sleepers, was constructed around the turntable. When piloting declined, the turntable was used less frequently, although locomotives working into Garsdale from the Wensleydale route still used it until that line was closed in 1954. After this shot was taken the stockade was dismantled and the turntable itself was later removed for preservation at Keighley on the Worth Valley Railway.

Trevor Owen

Left top: It is unlikely that the photographer, who has a collection of memorable S&C line pictures, regards this shot as one of his best, but at least the motive power is quite remarkable! Here, a grimy LNER-designed A1 Class Pacific, No. 60154 *Bon Accord*, is seen approaching Ais Gill summit, in charge of a southbound freight, on a dreary day in June 1965. These machines were only rarely seen on the S&C line, so this is probably an extremely rare colour shot. *Bon Accord* was allocated to York shed at the time of the photograph. Another example of an A1 Class working over the S&C line occurred on 4th July 1964 when No. 60118 *Archibald Sturrock* worked a Gourock to Leicester special. Sadly, the careers of these modern and quite impressive locomotives were ended long before they were life-expired. No. 60154 entered service in September 1949 and only lasted until October 1965. Towards the end of their lives A1s could be observed on a variety of mundane duties, such as that seen here. *Brian Magilton*

Left bottom: The majestic backdrop of snow-flecked Wild Boar Fell and Mallerstang Common, clouds scudding rapidly across the sky and a 'Black Five' producing a splendid smoke effect ... what more could a railway photographer wish for? Despite the strenuous climb all of the way from Ormside, No. 44795 still has steam to spare as it approaches the summit. What better testament to these excellent locomotives could there be? *A.E.R. Cope/Colour-Rail*

Most photographs of trains approaching Ais Gill summit from the north are taken from the western side of the line, but for a change, this picture was taken from the eastern side of the tracks. It shows Stanier Class 5MT 4-6-0 No. 45363 doing battle with the final few hundred yards of the demanding 1 in 100 gradient with a southbound van train on the glorious morning of 26th August 1966. The vehicles visible in this study are four-wheeled short-wheelbase vans, known to railwaymen as 'vanfits', which were notoriously unstable at high speed and therefore restricted to 45mph. They were once an everyday sight up and down the country, but have long since been consigned to the history books. The bridge carries the Moorcock to Kirkby Stephen road over the railway.

Roy Hobbs

The hard work is over for the crew of BR Standard Class 9F No. 92110, which has just breasted the summit with an empty Widnes to Long Meg mineral train, and they can relax as the trains drifts downhill. In fact, the enginemen will be able to take it relatively easy for the rest of the trip, because the gradient will be in their favour for nearly all of the way to Long Meg sidings, near Lazonby. The return journey, however, with a very heavy loaded train would have been a totally different proposition! The 'Long Megs', as they were generally referred to, were the star turns during the last years of steam over the S&C line and were consequently widely photographed. Towards the end of the steam era many locomotives were in a parlous state and frequently struggled on the unrelenting climb to Ais Gill. On one famous occasion a Stanier Class 8F, working one of those trains, was chronically short of steam and had to stop to raise steam on a number of occasions, taking almost fifty minutes to cover the seven miles from Kirkby Stephen to Ais Gill. A great spectacle for lineside observers, but an ordeal for the engine's crew. *Brian Magilton*

A short southbound freight, hauled by BR Standard Class 7P6F 'Britannia' Pacific No. 70032 *Tennyson,* crosses Ais Gill viaduct on 14th September 1967. At this time steam traction was rapidly being replaced by diesels on S&C line freight workings, and such sights as this became history at the end of December 1967 when steam working at Carlisle finished and Kingmoor shed was closed. The last ordinary steam working from Carlisle was reportedly the 1.10pm 'pick up' freight to Skipton on 30th December 1967, powered by 'Britannia' No. 70045 *Lord Rowallan.* *John Scrace*

Tennyson passes the photographer and heads towards Ais Gill summit which is less than a mile away. No. 70032 was built at Crewe Works, being out-shopped in December 1952. It was one of a small batch of 'Britannias' initially allocated to Holyhead for use on the London services, but they were found to have insufficient coal capacity for such a long run and were soon moved to Longsight where they were employed on the Manchester to London expresses. When these trains were dieselised, *Tennyson* was transferred across the city of Manchester to Trafford Park shed and a further move was later made to Willesden. It was withdrawn from Carlisle Kingmoor a few days after this shot was taken. Indeed, this may have been its last revenue-earning journey, who knows?

John Scrace

A northbound freight coasts downhill from Ais Gill summit past Mallerstang Common behind converted Crosti-boilered Class 9F No. 92021 on 22nd August 1967. By this date few of these distinctive machines remained in service, so, despite the locomotive's extremely grimy condition, it must have been a very welcome sight for the photographer. Ten Class 9Fs were built with Franco-Crosti boilers at Crewe Works in 1955, the aim of which was to increase the locomotives' thermal efficiency by diverting exhaust gases from the smokebox to heat boiler feed water in a pre-heater drum beneath the main boiler. The exhaust gases were then released to the atmosphere from a chimney positioned alongside the boiler, a most unorthodox arrangement that made these engines look very different from ordinary locomotives. In service the Crosti boilers, which had been developed in Italy, failed to produce the savings claimed by the inventor and the locomotives were soon modified for conventional operation. No. 92021 lasted in traffic for a further three months after this picture was taken and was later broken-up for scrap in Scotland.

Alan Chandler

A vintage view from the down platform of Kirkby Stephen West station showing an afternoon stopping train entering behind Stanier Class 5MT No. 44674 on 4th September 1954. The train comprises of three LMSR-designed coaches in carmine and cream livery, two vans and a milk tank wagon on the rear. Note the ancient MR sign on the right of the shot, while part of the tiny goods yard and cattle dock can be seen on the left. Goods facilities were withdrawn from 28th September 1964. The signal box, partially visible on the left, dated from 1894 and remained in use until 27th October 1974, when it was replaced by a BR standard-type box recovered from Kendal.

Neil Davenport

Alberta's swan song? During the summer of 1967, as mentioned elsewhere in this album, Stanier 'Jubilee' 4-6-0 No. 45562 *Alberta* made numerous sorties over the S&C line and gave considerable pleasure to many steam aficionados. It had been allocated to Holbeck shed, Leeds, where steam traction finished at the end of September 1967. But it seems that *Alberta* was granted a temporary stay of execution in order to work a railtour from the West Riding to Carlisle on 7th October. The train's outward journey was via the West Coast Main Line and, most appropriately, it returned via the S&C line where 'Jubilee' class locomotives had been a familiar sight for many years. In this picture, No. 45562 glints in the evening sun as it rounds the curve at Smardale on the return run. It is likely that this was *Alberta*'s last public appearance as it was condemned during the following month.

Maurice Burns

In this interesting scene at Appleby, taken on 6th August 1962, Fowler Class 4MT 2-6-4T No. 42304 is depicted shunting some six-wheeled milk tank wagons. The Appleby plant of the Express Dairy Company was situated on the up side of the line about half a mile south of Appleby station, and at one time was a source of much railborne traffic. The legend 'Milk for London' was displayed at the creamery in huge letters for the benefit of railway passengers. The siding on which No. 42304 is standing has long since been removed, while the partially visible Appleby West signal box, which dated from 1890, was taken out of use in October 1973. Another well-known feature at Appleby, which has also disappeared, is the substantially-built water tank, in the background.

Michael Allen

Bystanders appear to be transfixed as gleaming LMSR Class 6P5F 'Jubilee' No. 45562 *Alberta* rolls into Appleby station with the 6.40am SO Birmingham to Glasgow train on 26th August 1967. During the summer of 1967 *Alberta*, and sister engine No. 45593 *Kolhapur,* were booked to work this train, or the 9.20am SO St. Pancras to Glasgow, over the S&C line and were maintained in sparkling condition by Holbeck (Leeds) shed. The use of these locomotives rekindled happy memories for many enthusiasts of the days when 'Jubilees' appeared regularly on the line and the exploits of these two engines, which were the last survivors of their class on BR, brought considerable pleasure to many observers. At the end of September 1967 steam traction ceased in the Leeds area, and *Alberta* made a commemorative journey over the S&C line on 30th September hauling a Hunslet to Carlisle freight. There had been hopes that this machine - the pride of Holbeck shed - would be privately preserved, but sadly these were dashed when it was found to have badly worn tyres and No. 45593 was saved instead.

John Phillips

Left: Fowler 2-6-4T No. 42301 is illustrated leaving Armathwaite with the 6.05pm Carlisle to Appleby stopping train on the almost cloudless evening of 19th April 1963. The locomotive's tank sides and bunker are in quite clean condition, but the efforts of the cleaners do not appear to have been extended to the rest of the engine! This area may lack the grandeur of other parts of the S&C line, but the delightful sections around Armathwaite, with its outstanding views of the meandering river Eden, has an appeal all of its own. No. 42301 was one of a class of 125 locomotives which was designed by Sir Henry Fowler and constructed between 1927 and 1934. This particular example was the second engine to be built, appearing in December 1927. It lasted in traffic for a further six months after this shot was taken. *Robert Leslie*

Right: Stanier 'Black Five' No. 45063 leaves Armathwaite with the 8.05am Carlisle to Hellifield stopping train on Whit Monday, 3rd June 1963. The sun is shining brightly which augurs well for a nice day: most unusual for a Bank Holiday! Note that the train is made up of at least five coaches, a relatively heavy formation for a S&C line local working. Perhaps the LMR were anticipating some Bank Holiday crowds! *Robert Leslie*

A light sprinkling of snow lying on nearby fields helps to create a striking image as Stanier Class 6P5F 'Jubilee' 4-6-0 No. 45741 *Leinster* climbs the 1 in 132 gradient towards Cotehill with a Durranhill to Skipton freight on 2nd February 1963. No. 45741 was one of the final examples of its class to be constructed, emerging from Crewe Works in December 1936. It remained in service for less than a year after this portrait was taken, being condemned in January 1964. Cotehill is one of the S&C line's forgotten stations, being closed as long ago as 1952 and demolished soon afterwards.   *Robert Leslie*

Above: A Workington to London express passes Silverdale station in charge of Stanier Class 6P5F 'Jubilee' 4-6-0 No. 45552 *Silver Jubilee* in August 1962. This locomotive was an impostor, because it started its career as LMSR No. 5642 and changed its identity to LMSR No. 5552 in April 1935 to mark the Silver Jubilee of King George V. The new No. 5552 was given a high gloss black livery with plated raised cabside numerals and nameplates, the special numerals and nameplates being retained until the engine was withdrawn in September 1964. In addition, it had highly polished buffers and chrome fittings which included the top feed cover, steam pipes, boiler bands and handrails. Impostor or not, it must once have been a quite splendid sight, in sad contrast to its filthy condition in this shot.
Neil Thexton

Left: A work-stained Class WD 2-8-0, No. 90533, plods wearily past Cumwhinton with a Kingmoor to Skipton freight on 1st June 1963. A total of 935 of these heavy freight workhorses was built, of which 733 came into BR ownership. They could be seen on most BR regions, including the Southern Region for a short time, and were especially associated with the industrial north of England. No. 90533, originally WD No. 77062, was one of the small contingent employed on the Southern Region in early BR days, based at Feltham shed on the edge of south-west London. Following its stint at Feltham, it moved to Newton Heath shed, Manchester, where it was destined to spend most of its BR career.
Robert Leslie

This picture, it must be admitted, has been published before, but who could resist the temptation to include this absolutely stunning silhouette study of 'Black Five' No. 44781 crossing Arnside viaduct. The locomotive was powering the 8.28pm Barrow to Preston van train on 2nd August 1968, the last weekday of BR steam traction. The engine spent the following day at Lostock Hall shed being prepared for railtour duty on Sunday 4th August, when it was paired with BR Standard 'Britannia' Pacific No. 70013 *Oliver Cromwell* for part of the day. A week later it was one of the locomotives selected to haul the last BR steam train over the S&C line. Regrettably, these exploits did not ensure its long-term survival, because it was later used in a film during which it was wrecked and subsequently broken-up for scrap. A tragic end for, what had become, an historic locomotive.   *John Scrace*

A young man in swimming trunks dashes across the sands, apparently oblivious to the presence of BR Standard Class 4MT No. 75048 crossing Arnside viaduct with a short freight during the last few days of steam working in August 1968. Perhaps he was a railway enthusiast running for his camera! The Lake District fells provide a most pleasant, distant backdrop. The 1,300 feet-long viaduct across the Kent estuary was renewed in the 1880s and completely rebuilt during the First World War due to the salt water having damaged the cast iron columns. *Derek Huntriss*

An everyday scene at Grange-over-Sands as a rather dirty Stanier Class 6P5F 'Jubilee', No. 45670 *Howard of Effingham*, coasts into the station with an unidentified westbound train on 8th July 1960. The station here is situated adjacent to the shore, most convenient for enthusiastic holiday-makers, and in fact the quite scenic line between Arnside and Kents Bank stations is rarely out of sight of Morecambe Bay. Despite is undoubted attractions, this route has been somewhat neglected by railway photographers and has certainly never reached the popularity of the stretch between Dawlish and Teignmouth! The promontory in the middle-distance, on the right, is Holme Island. *John Langford*

The 6.40am Euston to Workington train is pictured leaving Grange-over-Sands behind Ivatt Class 4MT 2-6-0 No. 43000 on 3rd September 1962. The locomotive has plenty of steam to spare and is 'blowing off' as it skirts the promenade. This train was clearly designed for the most determined travellers with plenty of time on their hands, the marathon journey from London to Workington taking more than ten hours! No. 43000 was built at Horwich Works in December 1947, just before nationalisation of the railway system, and was one of the few members of the class to be painted in LMSR livery. It remained in service until September 1967.

Roy Patterson

Stanier Class 4MT 2-6-4T No. 42447 stands amidst the splendid surroundings of Ulverston station while working the 10.20am Morecambe Promenade to Lake Side (Windermere) train on 5th August 1962. The station buildings date from 1872-74 and were designed by Paley and Austin of Lancaster who were responsible for other stations in the area. The structures were built in an Italianate style, the main building boasting a tall clocktower and elaborate roof, while the platform canopies have richly monogrammed iron work. Perhaps the station's most unusual feature, though, is the down line which has platform faces on both sides. This was apparently to facilitate easy exchange between main line and the erstwhile Lake Side branch services.

Michael Allen

In the 1960s railway enthusiasts were a hardy breed, willing to suffer the rigours of travelling in a bouncy, rattling four-wheeled goods brake van if it meant they could travel over routes not usually traversed by passenger trains. Many such trips were organised by societies and, judging by the number of faces visible in this shot, they were extremely popular despite (or perhaps because of!) the discomfort involved. The train depicted is the 'Furness Rail Tour', which ran on 2nd September 1967, covering many obscure branches in the immediate area of Barrow-in-Furness before venturing along the Lakeside and Sandside branches. In this picture it is seen traversing the little-known Barrow avoiding line, near Park South, *en route* to the Lakeside branch. Motive power is 'Black Five' No. 45134, which had been cleaned up for the occasion. The train terminated in the evening at Carnforth, from where many participants no doubt returned home in an equally bouncy d.m.u!

Peter Fitton

Top left: Class 3F 0-6-0 No. 52501 glows in the evening sunshine with an enthusiasts' special at Workington Central station in September 1954. The train was the Stephenson Locomotive Society's 'West Cumberland Rail Tour'. This is a very rare shot of one of these engines, which were designed by Pettigrew for the Furness Railway and introduced in 1913. They weighed 42tons 13cwt and had a tractive effort of 21,935lbs. At the time of this photograph a handful of these locomotives were still in service at Workington and Moor Row sheds, where they were presumably employed on local freight and shunting work.
C. Banks collection/Colour-Rail

Bottom left: During the last years of steam, enthusiasts flocked to Shap to witness main line action, but very few visited the Carlisle to Barrow line where there was still considerable steam activity, a wide variety of scenery and some interesting single line sections. The railways around Workington must be some of the least photographed in Great Britain, perhaps due to the area's rather unappealing industrial image. In steam days it was dominated by heavy industry, principally steel and coal, for which Risehow colliery's two huge pit waste tips, in the background of this picture, provide ample testament. The scene is near Siddick Junction, just outside Workington, and Ivatt Class 4MT 2-6-0 No. 43027 is depicted working a southbound coal train in November 1967 during the last months of steam working on this line. *Derek Huntriss*

The 'real' Clapham Junction (as opposed to the one in south London!) is seen in this illustration which shows Hughes/Fowler Class 5MT 2-6-0 No. 42851 rounding the curve from the Lancaster direction with an unidentified passenger train on a stormy 28th July 1962. The other line is the route to Ingleton and Low Gill which had been reduced to 'freight only' operation by the time of the picture. The latter line was the first on the scene, the North Western Railway being incorporated in June 1846 to build a line from Skipton to Low Gill via Settle, Ingleton and Kirkby Lonsdale, with a branch to Lancaster. The company was unofficially known as the 'Little North Western' to avoid confusion with the much larger London & North Western Railway. The opening from Skipton to Low Gill took place on 30th July 1849. The section from Clapham Junction to Lancaster via Wennington was opened on 1st June 1850.

John Langford

Top left: The Morecambe portion of a Leeds to Morecambe/Carnforth train is seen making a smoky departure from Wennington behind unrebuilt 'Patriot' 4-6-0 No. 45505 *The Royal Army Ordnance Corps* on 24th April 1962. This locomotive was built at Crewe Works in July 1932 and lasted in traffic until withdrawn in June 1962, a few weeks after this photograph was taken. *Peter Fitton*

Bottom left: A picture taken at Wennington on 28th July 1962, in more prosperous times, when it was still a fairly important country junction station. The train on the left, with Stanier 'Black Five' No. 45445 in charge, is the Carnforth portion of the 1.55pm Leeds City to Carnforth/Morecambe Promenade, consisting of three LMSR corridor coaches. On the right 2-6-4T No. 42457 waits for the line to clear, before backing-down onto the Morecambe section of the train consisting of five non-corridor carriages. The 'little' North Western Railway's line from Clapham to Lancaster 'arrived' at Wennington in 1850 which remained a quiet rural station until the line to Carnforth was opened by the Furness & Midland Railway Joint Railway in 1867. The pattern of services was considerably altered when the Morecambe line was closed from 3rd January 1966, and all trains diverted to run via Carnforth. *John Langford*

Pictured high up in the Pennines, a Newcastle to Blackpool train crosses Belah viaduct on 12th August 1961. Motive power is provided by Ivatt Class 4MT 2-6-0 No. 43126 being piloted by BR Standard Class 3MT 2-6-0 No. 77002. This was an outstanding line which took trains across the roof of England, and on a clear day views from the carriage window could be quite magnificent. The route was promoted in 1857 as the South Durham & Lancashire Railway to connect Barnard Castle with Tebay, and opened four years later. Its main purpose was to move mineral traffic, coke, westwards from Durham to ironworks in Cumberland and iron ore eastwards to County Durham. The line attained a height of 1,370 feet above sea level at Stainmore summit, the highest point on a main line railway in England. A branch from Kirkby Stephen to Penrith was opened in the early 1860s. The remarkable Belah viaduct, designed by Thomas Bouch, consisted of sixteen spans and was 196 feet high.

Trevor Owen

Left: A reduction in the heavy mineral traffic, for which the Stainmore route was built, coupled with the substantial maintenance costs of the route, prompted BR to seek closure in the early 1960s. The Kirkby Stephen to Tebay section had already been closed to regular passenger trains in December 1952, although it remained open for freight and seasonal passenger workings. The line's freight trains could be easily diverted to other routes, and all-year-round passenger traffic was negligible, just three local trains a day (in each direction) being advertised in the summer 1960 timetable. The last scheduled passenger trains ran in January 1962, but a remnant of the line survived at the western end to serve Merrygill quarry and an army base at Warcop. In this shot the ruins of the former Kirkby Stephen East station form a rather depressing background as Ivatt Class 4MT No. 43040 trundles past with some wagons for the quarry on 23rd April 1965. *Trevor Owen*

Right: The old order on the Stainmore route! A former North Eastern Railway 0-6-0 (LNER Class J21) No. 65103 approaches Kirkby Stephen East station with a Penrith-bound train on 31st August 1954. Note the very short train which indicates the very sparse passenger traffic on offer even in the mid-1950s, when private cars were still very much a luxury and by no means as commonplace as they are today. There was a generous layout at Kirkby Stephen East consisting of a goods yard complete with cattle pens, carriage sidings, two signal boxes and a four-road engine shed. *Neil Davenport*

Many pictures of trains at Appleby West station have been published over the years but, for a change, here is a portrait of a train entering the much less photographed Appleby East station. Motive power is North Eastern Railway Worsdell-designed 0-6-0 No. 65064 and the train is presumably a Penrith to Darlington working which was photographed during the mid-1950s. The train has just passed a level crossing over a minor road, but the crossing is hidden from view. The chimney of Appleby East signal box, which controlled the level crossing, is just visible above the locomotive's cab roof. The station here consisted of only one platform, but there was a loop line and modest goods yard with a stone-built shed. This section of line was officially known as the Eden Valley Branch for many years, but when the Kirkby Stephen to Tebay line was closed to regular passenger traffic in 1952 it became the 'main line'.

Neil Davenport

Despite the closure of the Tebay to Kirkby Stephen line to advertised passenger traffic in the early 1950s, the route continued to witness passenger workings from the North East to Blackpool (and vice versa) on Saturdays only during the height of the summer. Curiously, these trains continued to run long after regular services had ceased and in this view a Blackpool to Newcastle train is depicted passing the disused station at Ravenstonedale on 12th August 1961. The locomotives are Ivatt Class 4MT No. 43056 piloting BR Standard Class 4MT No. 76050. One wonders if the gentleman and young lad standing on the platform realised how lucky they were to see a steam-hauled passenger train passing the former station. By this date only about thirty or so such workings a year operated, and the summer of 1961 was destined to be their last.

Trevor Owen

A most interesting illustration, taken at Tebay on 8th July 1960, showing Fairburn Class 4MT 2-6-4T No. 42673 waiting to depart from the up loop platform with the 2.45pm Durham to Ulverston train. The tank locomotive had just replaced Ivatt Class 2MT 2-6-0 No. 46458 which had brought the train across the Pennines via Barnard Castle. This train ran on alternate Fridays and operated principally for the benefit of miners going to convalesce at either Grange-over-Sands or Ulverston. In addition to traversing the magnificent Stainmore line, the train also ran over the little-known Hincaster Junction to Arnside route, which lost its advertised passenger service as long ago as 1953. Thus a fair proportion of the route used by this train was not open to regular passenger working.

John Langford

The Cockermouth, Keswick & Penrith Railway (CK&PR) ran from the industrial town of Workington through the northern valleys of lakeland to Penrith, on the West Coast Main Line. It was an outstanding line with breathtaking views of some of the best Lakeland scenery. The line was built primarily to convey freight traffic, pig-iron and iron ore eastwards and coke westwards, via the Stainmore route across the Pennines. It enabled the south Durham coal owners to compete on equal terms with those in the north of the county who had easy access to West Cumberland via the Newcastle to Carlisle line. The route was engineered by Thomas Bouch and consisted of 31 miles of single line, including no fewer than 135 bridges, which climbed to a summit of 889 feet above sea level just east of Troutbeck station. The line opened to freight in October 1864 and to passenger trains from 2nd January 1865. Most of the passenger services were taken over by d.m.u.s in the mid-1950s, so colour photographs of steam traction working over the route are uncommon. Here, Ivatt-designed Class 2MT 2-6-0 No. 46458, working tender-first, is seen climbing towards Troutbeck with the Royal Train on 22nd July 1966. The 'Royal' was run in connection with a visit to Keswick by HRH The Duke of Edinburgh.
Maurice Burns

No. 46458 is seen again, this time running into Troutbeck station with the train depicted in the previous shot. When the line was originally built the heavily-graded section between Troutbeck and Threlkeld was particularly difficult to work because trains were slowed due to the grades, and they consequently spent a long time in the section which disrupted traffic movements when the line was busy. This section was converted to double track in the 1890s, but by the date of this picture, 22nd July 1966, the route had been closed beyond Keswick and the double track section had apparently reverted to one operational single line, although the surplus, abandoned track was still *in situ* at this time.

Maurice Burns

The Stephenson/Manchester Locomotive Societies' 'Lakes & Fells Railtour' pauses at Keswick station on 2nd April 1966. This was the last steam-hauled train to traverse the section west of Keswick, which was closed a fortnight later. The tour started from Manchester and is reported to have been beset with problems, arriving back in the city at 1am, so participants are unlikely to have forgotten that trip in a hurry! Motive power over the Penrith to Workington section was a brace of Ivatt Class 2MT 'Moguls', Nos. 46458 and 46426.

J. Spencer Gilks

The Silloth branch has a rather unusual history, and was opened in two separate stages. The first section from Carlisle to Drumburgh was built on the course of the Carlisle canal which had been constructed in 1823 to link the 'Border City' with Port Carlisle, eleven miles distant. Unfortunately, the canal company soon got into financial difficulties and sought parliamentary approval to convert the canal into a railway line, which was given in August 1853. The route opened to goods traffic in May 1854 and to passengers a month later. The facilities at Port Carlisle were increasingly affected by silt, however, and it was decided to use the branch as a springboard for a new line from the intermediate station of Drumburgh to Silloth Bay, where the tidal conditions were more favourable and there was deeper water closer to the shore. This plan by the Carlisle & Silloth Bay Railway Company provoked a very hostile reaction from the Maryport & Carlisle Railway, the Maryport Harbour Trustees and local landowners, and was initially rejected by parliament. It was later approved, on 16th July 1855. The extension became involved in local politics, but even so went ahead, culminating in the opening on 28th August 1856. The railway company decided to develop Silloth to create a source of passenger revenue and invested heavily in new housing, a bathhouse, a gasworks and even a hotel. The North British Railway (NBR) operated steamers from Silloth to Liverpool and also used the port for goods for a while, and Silloth witnessed a period of relative prosperity in the 1860s, but the opening of the Settle & Carlisle line in 1876 gave the NBR a better outlet to England and it lost interest in Silloth. The line faded into obscurity and eventually lost its passenger service from 7th September 1964. It appears that the route was rarely visited by colour photographers, so this view of Ivatt Class 4MT 2-6-0 No. 43027 awaiting departure from Silloth with the 11.20am to Carlisle on 3rd August 1964 is probably something of a rarity. *Mike Hudson*

The Ulverston to Windermere (Lake Side) branch was promoted by the Furness Railway (FR) which obtained an Act of Parliament for the first section as far as Newby Bridge on 16th July 1866. The seven miles-long single track line had a double track triangular junction with the 'main line' 1½ miles east of Ulverston. Goods trains commenced as far as Newby Bridge on 23rd April 1869. The FR had its eye, of course, on the tourist potential of linking up with the lake steamers, but decided that using the existing steamer berth at Newby Bridge, which involved vessels negotiating the headwaters of the river Leven, was too risky and it was resolved to build a purpose-built quay at Lake Side. This was commissioned on 1st June 1869 and passenger services along the entire branch commenced on that date. During the period prior to the First World War tourist and excursion traffic on the branch grew steadily, but winter steamer services on the lake were withdrawn in the early 1920s, an event which presaged the decline of the branch's passenger trains. All-year-round services ceased from 26th September 1938 and were withdrawn altogether for most of the Second World War period. On 3rd June 1946 seasonal passenger services recommenced, but clearly this kind of service was vulnerable to BR's economy drive of the 1960s and the line was soon under threat. Passenger trains ran for the last time on 6th September 1965 and part of the route subsequently fell victim to a road improvement scheme. The northern section, however, survives as a steam-operated preserved line, so at least some of this particularly scenic route has been saved for posterity. The charming terminus at Lake Side is seen on 5th August 1962, with Lake Windermere and distant mountains providing a memorable backdrop.

Michael Allen

A beautifully turned-out unrebuilt 'Patriot' Class 6P5F 4-6-0, No. 45543 *Home Guard,* stands at Lake Side station at the head of a return excursion to Birmingham on 1st July 1956. The waters of Lake Windermere are hidden by the locomotive, but the tops of the fells which line the other side of the lake are just visible. No. 45543 was one of the last unrebuilt survivors of its type and was withdrawn in November 1962 when the sub-class was rendered extinct.
John Edgington

Photographed on the rather overcast day of 5th August 1962, Stanier Class 5MT No. 45258 approaches Haverthwaite with a passenger working which left Preston at 9.58am and conveyed through coaches from Blackpool Central. The Blackpool portion was booked to leave at 8.45am, so any holiday-makers desiring a day in the Lake District would have had to ask their landlady for a fairly early breakfast! Reaching Ulverston at 11.18am, the engine ran-round and departed tender-first at 11.29am to Lake Side. *Neil Thexton*

The ten miles-long branch line from Oxenholme to Windermere was promoted locally by the Kendal & Windermere Railway Company, which was incorporated on 30th June 1845. The section as far as Kendal was opened on 22nd September 1846, this also being the date that the southern portion of the Lancaster & Carlisle Railway was opened. The branch opened throughout on 21st April 1847, a beautiful spring day. The event was a cause of much celebration in Windermere and at other intermediate points on the route. In May 1858 the local company entered a leasing arrangement with the Lancaster & Carlisle Railway, but negotiations were not concluded until after the latter had itself been swallowed up by the London & North Western Railway in late 1859. The Windermere branch mercifully escaped the Beeching economies of the 1960s and is still in operation today, being the only railway line into the heart of the Lake District. In this portrait, taken on 1st September 1964, Fairburn Class 4MT No. 42680 is seen running into Oxenholme station with the 9.25am Windermere to London Euston. It would have been combined there with the 8.40am from Carlisle, the arrival time in the Capital being 4.20pm.

Alan Robey

The chalked inscription on the smokebox door of Class 5MT No. 44709 says it all 'Farewell from Windermere and Kendal - Well Done Steam'. Almost needless to say, this scene was recorded on the last day of steam working on the branch, 2nd August 1968, and depicts the last steam hauled freight approaching Burneside. Note the two 'guards' travelling in the brake van: let us hope the real guard checked their tickets before they boarded! Many locomotives in action on the final weekend of steam traction were given special cleaning treatment by enthusiasts, but unfortunately No. 44709 does not seem to have been a recipient of this lavish attention.

David Clark

Right: The attractive, largely stone-built station building at Staveley is depicted in this picture, which was taken on 29th August 1965. The view is looking north, towards Windermere. Note the wooden platform extension and gas lighting. Naturally, the premises are decorated with a full set of LMR 'sausage' station signs in the regional maroon colours. Between Staveley and Windermere the line reached a summit, almost 500ft. above sea level, at Blackmoss. *Michael Allen*

Left: An almost timeless, everyday scene in Windermere goods yard, as Class 5MT No. 44894 simmers gently, presumably after arrival with a freight working which conveyed domestic coal for the local merchant. His lorry is waiting to be loaded with the sacks sitting on the ground, before he can set off on his delivery round. But the group of young men on the left of the shot give a clue that this apparently routine operation was photographed during the last week of steam traction. It was very much the end of an era, and for many railwaymen the end of a way of life going back almost 150 years. This picture was taken on Thursday 1st August 1968, the penultimate weekday of standard gauge BR steam. *David Clark*

Fairburn-designed 2-6-4T No. 42118 simmers at the buffer stops at Windermere after arrival with the 3.30pm train from Oxenholme on 29th August 1965. Note the magnificent row of ornate platform lamps. In time-honoured fashion, the fireman has just retrieved the headlamp from the front of the locomotive. By this date the LMSR-designed 2-6-4Ts were being rapidly thinned-out by withdrawals, as line closures and the introduction of more modern motive power took their toll. This may account for the group of young men on the platform who appear to be railway enthusiasts. If they had just enjoyed a ride behind No. 42118 it may have been their last behind that locomotive, because it was withdrawn from traffic within a few weeks of this picture being taken. Indeed this may have been its last day in service, who knows?

Michael Allen